PUBLISHED BY BRINKTANK LLC

Library of Congress Cataloging-in-Publication Data
ISBN: 978-0-9960644-3-9

Special Sales
Brinktank Books are available at special discounts for bulk purchases for sales promotions or premiums. Special editions, including personalized covers, excerpts of existing books, and corporate imprints, can be created in large quantities for special needs.
Sadiq would also be happy to conduct a book signing and/or presentation for your school or organization.

For more information, write to:
info@Millionaire-Manners.com

For more information visit us at:
www.Millionaire-Manners.com

PRINTED IN THE UNITED STATES OF AMERICA
15 14 13 12 11   10 9 8 7 6 5 4 3 2 1

This book is dedicated to my Father,
my sons and all my other sons,
who I am not related to by blood.
Our family is one.

Boy, Get That Crust Off Your Face!

Little Saire Learns about Personal Hygiene

written by Sadiq Ali
illustrated by Giedre Senlūniene

MALCOLM X SCHOOL
A+

There was a little boy named Saire. He lives in the city with his Mom and Dad and Grandmother. Little Saire is a great student. He is in the 4th grade and loves school. He is in the Chess Club and on the Basketball team at his school. He does all his homework, listens to his parents, helps his Grandmother and even volunteers on the weekends! He is what you would call, "a pillar of his community" and a busy young man!

Saire is very *fussy* yet he loves *winning* and being the best! There is one problem, though. He rushes in the morning and he forgets to take care himself *properly*.

Sometimes his clothes are *wrinkled* his hair isn't brushed and sometimes he even forgets to brush his teeth! *Ewwwwwww!*

Saire is smart, funny and good to hang out with, but one day his friends stopped hanging out with him *one by one.*

He asked them to *study* together, and they made up *excuses*. He asked them to play outside and they told him they had chores to do, but he knew they *hated* chores! Saire didn't know what was *wrong*!

Saire was *stumped* on why his friends decided to stop hanging out with him. So he went to his favorite thinking place in his *backyard* behind his house and sat under the tree.

Then he started thinking...

Hmmmmmmm...

As Saire sat and thought about why he had been *losing* friends, he started asking himself questions.

"Hmmmm... am I being a good friend?"
"Yup," he thought.

"Have I been bullying anyone?"
"Nope," he said to himself.
"I never bully people."

He thought and thought and *thought!*

Suddenly, Saire had a thought that hit him like a bolt of lightning! He remembered having a conversation with his Grandmother one day as she saw him rushing to get ready for school and looking very messy as he did it. She told him: "Boy, get that crust off your face!" She went on to tell him that "people are always judging you, Grandson, and sometimes it's not fair. You must always put your best foot forward to the world everyday, and it starts with how you take care of yourself and how you look!"

Saire couldn't believe he had *forgotten* these important lessons he had heard before. But sometimes the voice of Grandma is the strongest! He *immediately* decided that this was the possible reason his friends *stopped* hanging out with him!

He was excited to get to the bottom of the *mystery*. He even had some ideas on how to fix it.

The next *morning*, Saire woke up extra early to get *ready* for school.

He started by *brushing* his teeth while he hummed his favorite song! He also remembered being told to brush for at least *60 seconds* and humming a song helped him do that.

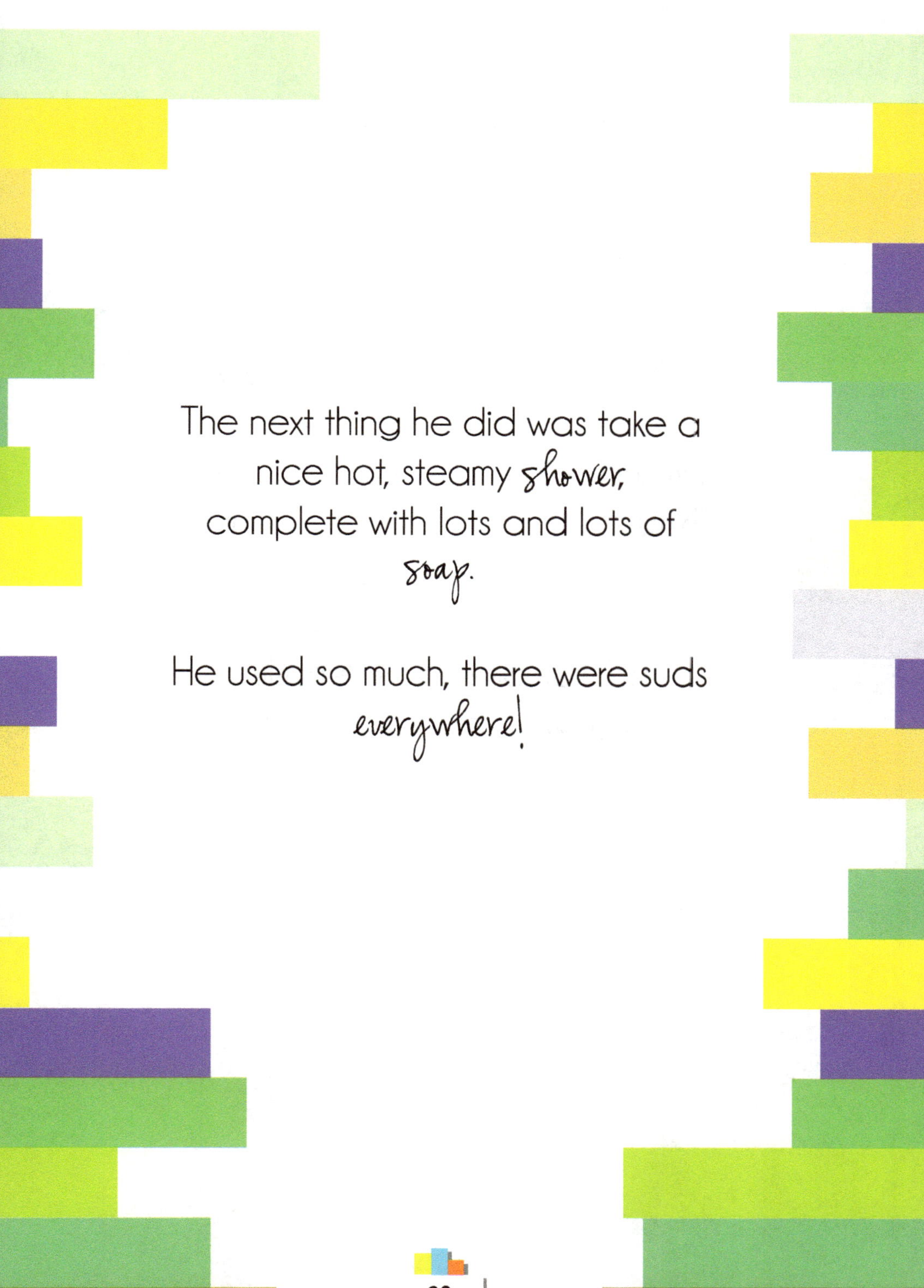

The next thing he did was take a nice hot, steamy shower, complete with lots and lots of soap.

He used so much, there were suds everywhere!

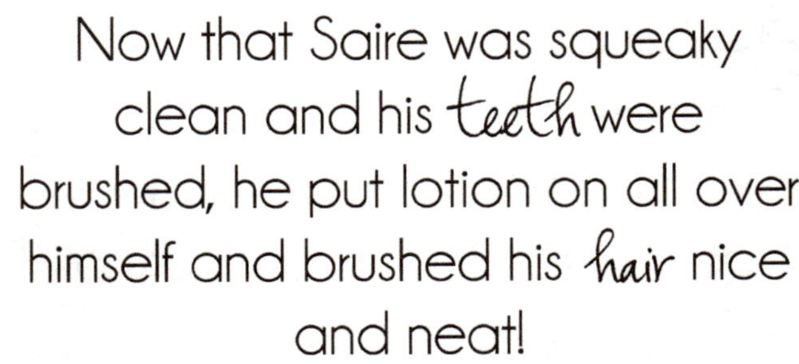

Now that Saire was squeaky clean and his teeth were brushed, he put lotion on all over himself and brushed his hair nice and neat!

He was already feeling like a million bucks! Or kind of like a superhero!

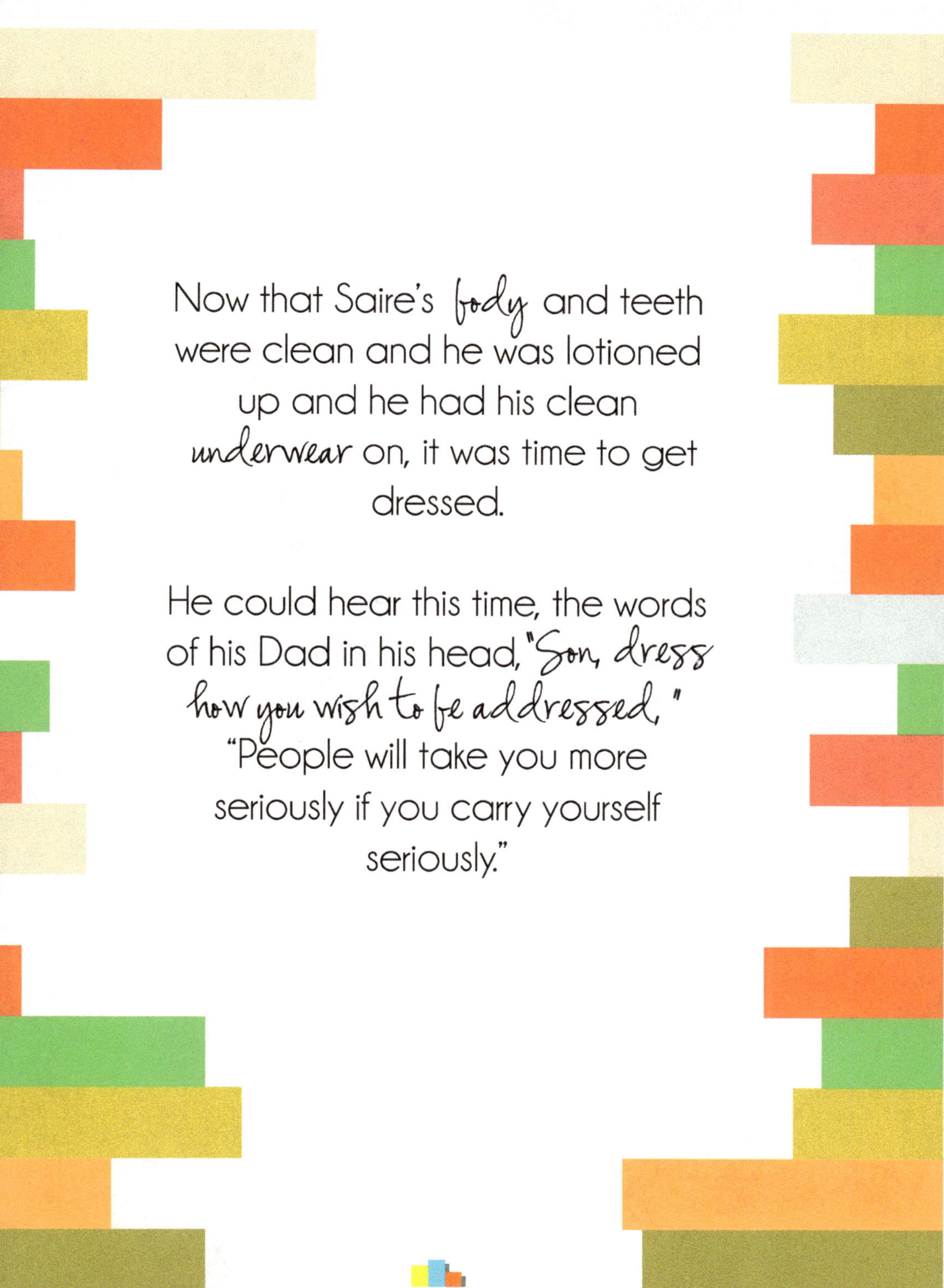

Now that Saire's *body* and teeth were clean and he was lotioned up and he had his clean *underwear* on, it was time to get dressed.

He could hear this time, the words of his Dad in his head, "*Son, dress how you wish to be addressed,*" "People will take you more seriously if you carry yourself seriously."

Until now, Saire never knew what those words meant. But now he had an idea.

He then found his favorite outfit and did something he hadn't done in a while - he ironed all his clothes! But he had to make sure he didn't burn a hole in them!

He didn't and now he was ready for school!

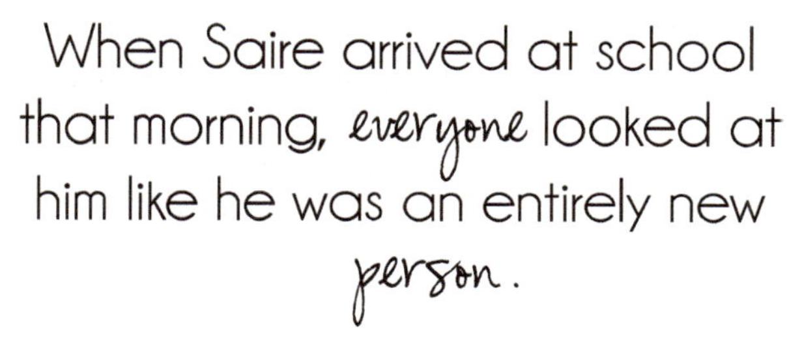

When Saire arrived at school that morning, *everyone* looked at him like he was an entirely new *person*.

And you know what, *he felt* like a new person too!

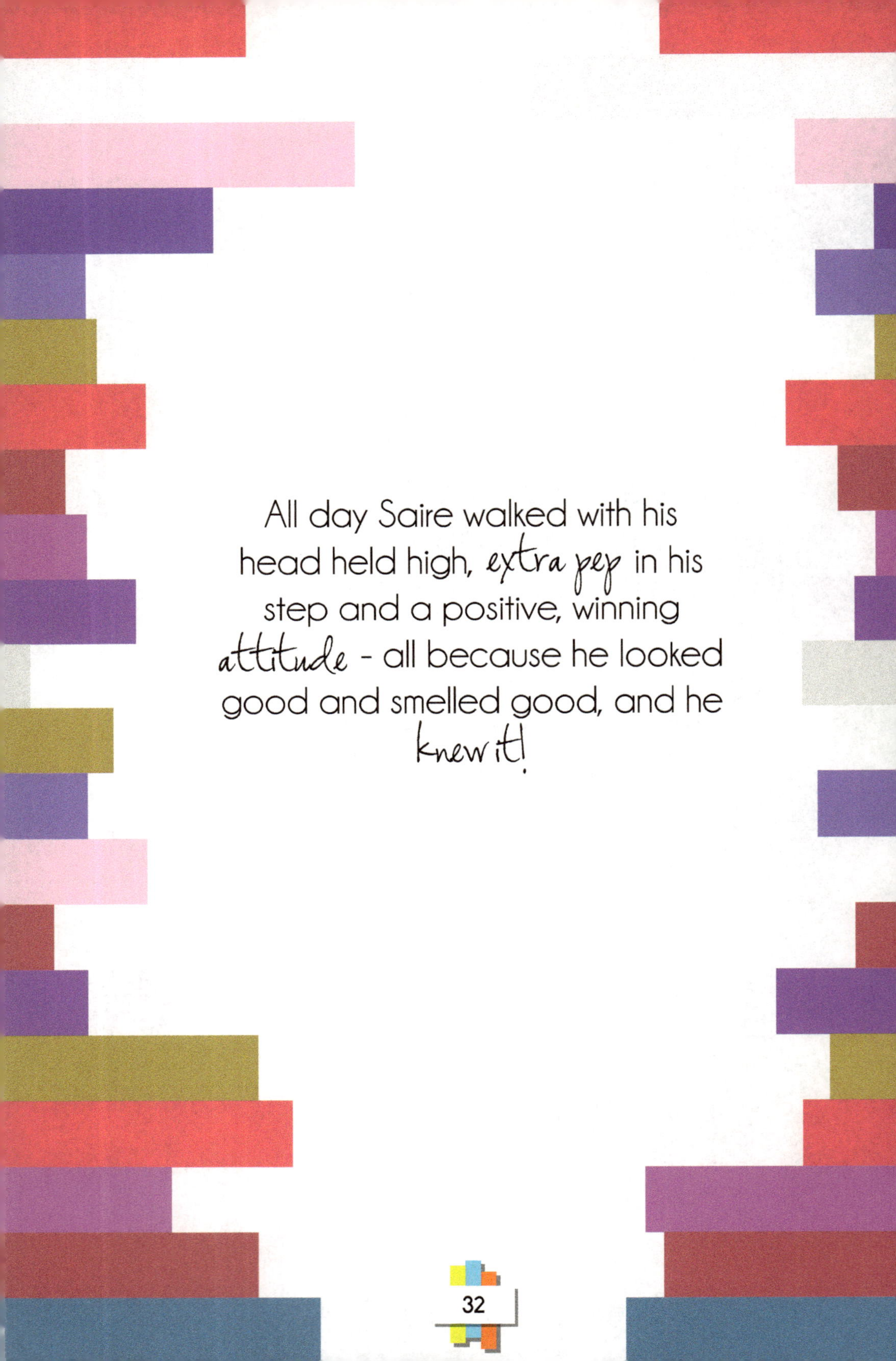

All day Saire walked with his head held high, *extra pep* in his step and a positive, winning *attitude* - all because he looked good and smelled good, and he *knew it!*

Saire was having a great day
and *finally* the moment arrived
that he had been waiting
for - seeing all his *friends*.

But this time instead of them
avoiding him, they rushed over
to him *excited* to see him!

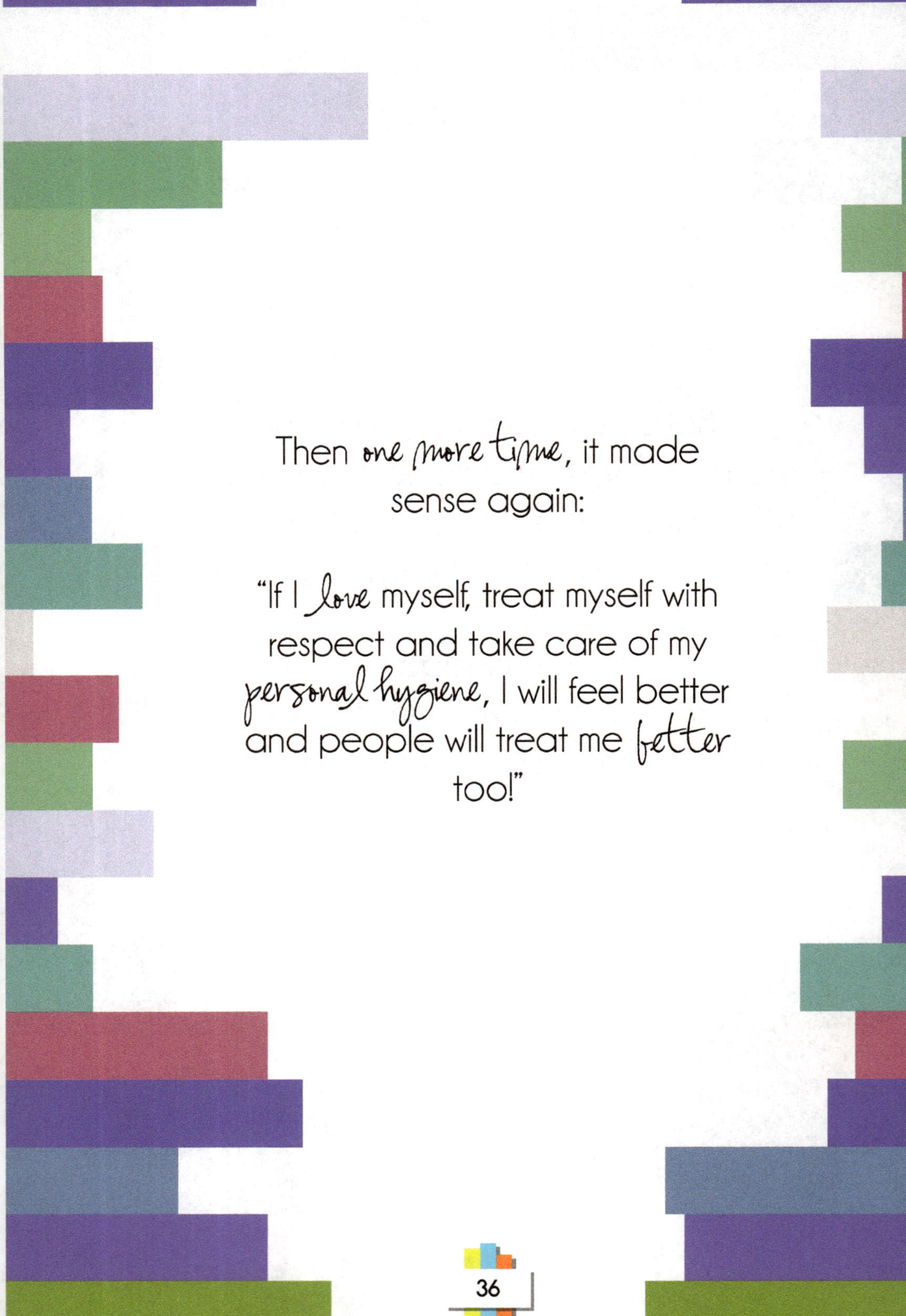

Then *one more time*, it made sense again:

"If I *love* myself, treat myself with respect and take care of my *personal hygiene*, I will feel better and people will treat me *better* too!"

MALCOLM X SCHOOL

Saire's Personal Hygiene Tips

Every morning you should:

1. Brush your teeth while humming the ABC song! That way you get all the germs and bacteria out of your mouth. Then if you have time, floss too!

2. Shower and wash your face! You can do this either at night or in the morning. If you shower at night, don't forget to wash your face in the morning. In the shower make sure you wash all the stinky spots!

3. Comb or brush your hair! And don't forget your hair oil!

4. Put lotion on your hands, body and face. In the winter, this will protect your skin.

5. Make sure your clothes aren't wrinkled! If you're old enough, you can iron them yourself, and if not, ask an adult to help you.

6. Clean your shoes before you leave the house.

7. Put a smile on your face! This is your best asset!

What tips would you add in?

Get your copy of Millionaire Manners *today!*

Visit: www.Millionaire-Manners.com/shop

The Live Weekly *Success* Call for Young People!

Visit: www.Millionaire-Manners.com/MentorMonday

MILLIONAIRE MANNERS ACADEMY

MILLIONAIRE MANNERS ACADEMY PRESENTS

MENTOR MONDAY

THE LIVE WEEKLY SUCCESS CALL FOR MENTORS, MENTEES, PARENTS, TEACHERS, STUDENTS AND MORE!

712-775-7031 // Meeting ID: 876-676#

AND JOIN OUR FREE REMINDER SERVICE: CALL REMINDERS, EVENT ALERTS, RESOURCES, INFORMATION, MOTIVATION & INSPIRATION! TEXT @MILMANNERS TO 81010 NOW!

EVERY MONDAY 8PM

FEATURING:
- Life hacks
- School hacks
- Confidence building
- Live Q&A session every week

AND more!

BROADCASTING LIVE ON Periscope WEEKLY AT 8PM // @MLLNREManners

/MillionaireManners @MillionaireManners @MLLNREManners millionaire-manners.com

Sadiq Ali, MBA is a proud Morgan State Alum and the founder of Millionaire Manners Academy, a training organization that focuses on leadership, life skills and career readiness through a framework of excellent interpersonal relationships. Sadiq has been recognized as a human potential and development expert, etiquette guru and customer service master who has worked up and down the east coast and formerly in corporate America.

With a heavy emphasis on self-esteem development, relationship building and youth empowerment, Sadiq has managed to motivate and redirect some of the most troubled youth and formerly incarcerated citizens.

The national recognition for The Young Gentlemen's Institute, awards and the like, though, pale in comparison to his favorite jobs which are husband, father and son. He enjoys spending time with his wife and four children, still attempting to play basketball and riding his motorcycle.

Through everything, Sadiq is determined to leave a lasting legacy and for us all to be better today than we were yesterday.

To have Sadiq come and speak at your school or organization, email or call us!

E-mail: info@millionaire-manners.com
Phone: 1-877-958-4009

Stay in touch!

Twitter: @MLLNREManners
Instagram: @MillionaireManners
Facebook: /MillionaireManners
Youtube: Millionaire Manners TV
Periscope: @MLLNREManners
Web: www.millionaire-manners.com

CPSIA information can be obtained
at www.ICGtesting.com
Printed in the USA
BVHW051143300720
584765BV00001B/1